MW00657999

The

21-DAY GUIDE

to discovering your

PASSION,

developing your

PLAN

& defining your

PURPOSE

DR. LORENA NEWSON

The 21-Day Guide to Discovering Your Passion, Developing Your Plan & Defining Your Purpose

Dr. Lorena Newson

ISBN (Print Edition): 978-1-66787-260-5

ISBN (eBook Edition): 978-1-66787-261-2

© 2022. All rights reserved. No part of this publication may be reproduced, distributed, or transmitted in any form or by any means, including photocopying, recording, or other electronic or mechanical methods, without the prior written permission of the publisher, except in the case of brief quotations embodied in critical reviews and certain other noncommercial uses permitted by copyright law.

SELF-ASSESSMENT GUIDE

A Note From the Author

Greetings, thank you for purchasing "The 21-Day Guide to Discovering Your Passion, Developing Your Plan & Defining Your Purpose" workbook.

As you embark upon this journey of self-reflection and discovery, please plan to set aside 30 minutes each day over the next 21 days to complete the activities and journal assignments in this workbook.

I personally like to begin with the end in mind. Think about the reason for your purchase of this text as it is important for us to know our "WHY." If your WHY is to learn more about the things that you excel in, areas in which you are gifted/talented, or career choices that may better suit your personality, then you have identified a useful resource here. Use this workbook as a guide, a tool for planning and to help keep you focused on your goals. Take it with you daily, interact with it as often as possible, revisiting topics, updating information and reflecting on your entries. If you do not already have a journal, you will need one as part of the planning process and to supplement this workbook.

On your 21 day journey, you will notice that each day has a word associated with it. As part of your reflection time each day, please spend 1-2 minutes meditating on the word of the day and what it means to you. Think about how you will apply the word of the day each day of your life. Also, the recommended readings are meant to help bring clarity and focus to your life and reinforce the daily topics. Recommended readings can be used for references and make for the beginning of a vast self-development library.

Lastly, always remember to celebrate the small successes. Fulfilling your purpose is a process and journey, it doesn't happen over night. This workbook will assist you with every step of the planning process and you can expect to discover new areas of interest once completing this workbook. Good luck during your journey.

You can do it!

Dr. Lorena J.

TABLE OF CONTENTS

INTENTIONALITY DAY ONE

"The power of the personal mission statement lies in your vision and in a commitment to that vision, that purpose, and those principle-centered values."

-Stephen R. Covey

When we are children we have big hopes about what we want to achieve as adults, but when adulthood arrives, the issues of life can often knock us off our path. Maybe you grew up in a household where your parents worked a 9-5, never complained and that subconsciously became your standard. Maybe you are on your own, and don't mind working but your quality of life is suffering and you feel unfulfilled. The purpose of this workbook is to get you back on track if you have somehow wandered off the beaten path. Are you tired of the current status quo and ready to make some changes? Are you content with where you are in life but want to be intentional about the plans you make for your future? If so, this workbook is for you.

How much thought have you put into the work that you currently do for a living? How did you get here? Was it on purpose; on accident, or coincidence?

Please rate the following, on a scale of 1-10, I am satisified with the work that I do for a living. (Circle one)

1 2 3 4 5 6 7 8 9 10

WORD OF THE DAY

Intentionality: The fact of being deliberate or purposive.

ACTIVITY 1

In the past year, I have shown intentionality in my employment by taking the following 3 steps:

1. ______________________________

2. ______________________________

3. ______________________________

JOURNAL QUESTION: What is your personal mission statement? How does your current employment fit?

READING RECOMMENDATION: Rick Warren, The Purpose Driven Life: What on Earth Am I Here For? (2002)

PASSION-WORK DAY TWO

"Everything you could possibly need is available to you in the full measure you could ever desire it."
-T.D. Jakes

After reflecting, are you content with where you are currently in your personal life? Career? How about familial life? Todays activity will require you to find 3 things that you are passionate about. It is important that we integrate passion with wisdom. We may discover things that we are passionate about but are not talented in, possess strong skills in nor have the capacity to develop. These passions are more likely hobbies. For the purpose of this workbook, lets dig a little bit deeper. While hobbies may be fun for us, they may not necessarily increase the quality of our lives or others. When identifying our passion, we want to specifically note things that interest us with things that we do well. This is important because God would never call us to an area that we could not perform in. God calls us to perform in areas that we have capacity for. Where can you have the biggest impact? Reflect on the feedback that you have received from others when using your passion and interests to discover your purpose. If there is an area that you excel in, enjoy, and have been told that you do well in, more than likely, this should be the focus of your "passion-work".

Is there a connection between your passion and the work that you do for a living? If not, what are some ways you can begin to integrate your true passions into your daily life? Be sure to integrate the responses to the questions above into your journal entry for the day. It is important for us to tie our passion to our careers because we are innately results driven. Passion and commitment drive performance, and without it, our quality of work will suffer.

WORD OF THE DAY

Passion-Work: Finanically benefitting from work in which you excel or find pleasure in.

ACTIVITY 2

My personal and professional passions include the following:

1. ____

2. ____

3. ____

JOURNAL QUESTION: If money wasn't a factor, how would you fulfill your days?

READING RECOMMENDATION: T.D. Jakes, Reposition Yourself: Living a Life Without Limits (2008)

TALENT DAY THREE

"The first step toward success is identifying
your own leadership strengths."
-Dale Carnegie

Talent is a gift. Over time you can become good at things that you practice, even if they are not second nature to you. It is important to note that just because you can learn a behavior or skill over time, does not mean that you are gifted or talented in that area. Talents are God given. Some use their talents to generate income, other use their talents to edify themselves and others. If you can use your talent to generate income and build others up at the same time, you are on the right path. Purpose includes talent and God given abilities. When we are at our best and feel fulfilled, our attitudes are positive and we can give our best to others. We cannot pour from an empty cup!

Are you passionate about things that you are not gifted and talented in? When we are talented in our work, and passionate, often times it doesn't feel like work. This means that the loathing, don't want to get out of bed days, nothing to look forward to days, will be few and far between. When you are working towards your passion, you are focused on your goal. When you are focused on your goal, there are few things that can knock you off track. Like many others, you will have to balance the trials of life but the goals and desires never completely leave you. You may have to regroup a few times but it is important to find things that can refocus you when you get off track.

WORD OF THE DAY

Talent: A special natural ability or aptitude; a capacity for achievement or success.

ACTIVITY 3

List 3 areas that you are talented in. Circle each talent that you are passionate about.

1. ______________________________

2. ______________________________

3. ______________________________

JOURNAL QUESTION: How are your talents different/similar from your passions? Highlight the similarities in your journal and list ways that you can use both to generate income.

READING RECOMMENDATION: Walt F.J. Goodridge, Turn Your Passion into Profit (1999)

REFLECTION DAY FOUR

"The seed must be planted before it can grow. When the grain is ripe, it must be cut down and ground into flour. Before it can become bread, it must pass through the oven."

-Max Lucado

Now that you have identified your passions and talents, lets focus on your current "process." What drives you each morning that you wake up? Are you intrinsically motivated, fueled by your family responsibilities or focused on a specific goal? While reflecting, it is important to determine the difference between working to no end and working towards an end goal. This thinking requires a mental paradigm shift. Working with no end in mind, does not set us up for long term success. Sometimes we have to do what we have to do intermittently, but getting stuck there can be dangerous. What goals do you have each day? Do they serve a bigger picture?

Self-Reflection: It is important to take the time to self-reflect because often time, we simply get too busy to reflect. When reflection is not a priority, self-care may become virtually non-existent. Reflection helps us to keep things in perspective and to reprioritize our lives when necessary. It is easy to forget the end goal and get caught up in the moment performing routine tasks when we are not reflective. When routine tasks are not intentional and purposeful, we can look up one day and wonder where all of our time went. Routines can be good,but we have to be careful when they don't push us or propel us towards our purpose. Always consider the bigger picture and do a little each day. Starting with large overwhelming tasks is unrealistic and does not set us up for long term success.

WORD OF THE DAY

Reflection: A fixing of the thoughts on something; careful consideration.

ACTIVITY 4

List 3 things that motivate you on a daily basis.

1. ____________________

2. ____________________

3. ____________________

JOURNAL QUESTION: How are you utilizing the motivational factors above toward success?

READING RECOMMENDATION: Kenneth W. Thomas, Intrinsic Motivation at Work: What Really Drives Employee Engagement (2002)

COMMITMENT DAY FIVE

"No one can rise above mediocrity unless
he believes in his own ability to become
and to remain self-determining."
–Napoleon Hill

Passion as Service. Working as a service or civic duty, can be rewarding if you are a person intrinsically motivated by helping others and acts of service bring you a sense of need fulfilment. When we are innately passionate about the work that we do, often times it doesn't feel like work. Instead, it feels like we are fulfilling our lifes mission and calling. CEO of Berkshire Hathaway, Warren Buffet stated "Without passion, you don't have energy, and without energy you have nothing." Passion fuels our every day progress. Even on days that we don't feel like working, our passion can and will sustain us. Has your fire gone out? What are some things you can do to re-ignite your passion? At the beginning of each year, we often set goals for ourselves. Try this the next time you set your goals; establish quarterly check in point to chart your progress. Quarterly check in points can be used to regroup and refocus if necessary.

Any job that we do will require us to invest and sacrifice our time. Time assessments can be useful not only for how we utilize our time at work but also our time at home. For example, there are 168 hours in a week. While this may seem silly at first, it may be a good practice to journal your weekly routines to see where and how you measure up. After you factor in work time, travel time and sleep time, how many hours do you have remaining to schedule all of the things that you need to get done? There is time available, we just have to keep the commitments. Schedules help us all to stay on track.

WORD OF THE DAY

Commitment: The state or quality of being dedicated to a cause, activity or obligation.

ACTIVITY 5

List 3 things that you are currently committed to. Circle those aligned with your passion.

1.____

2.____

3.____

JOURNAL QUESTION: What parts of your current commitments align with your passion?

READING RECOMMENDATION: Mike Driggers, Managing Your Commitment: Why Doing What You Said You Would Do Long After You Said You Would Do It Brings Lasting Passion, Purpose, and Success (2016)

PERFECTIONIST DAY SIX

"We began to realize that if we wanted to
change the situation, we first had to change
ourselves. And to change ourselves effectively,
we first had to change our perceptions."

-Stephen R. Covey

We are often over ambitious when creating plans for our lives. While having a plan is commendable, we must ensure that our plans set us up for success. It is important to make plans that are realistic and allow us adequate time for fulfillment. We should also factor in trials of life and be prepared for the unexpected. We hardly account for the worst when goal setting but it is necessary to note that circumstances may arise temporarily that require our full time and attention. If we are not careful, we can allow these circumstances to thwart our focus and get us off track. When planning, we must build grace into our plans. We must understand that we are human and may have to make adjustments daily. We have to be flexible. When pursuing your passion, keep in mind that things will come up. How you successfully navigate things that are unexpected is equally as important as following your plan and accomplishing your goal.

A mindset of perfection can hinder process. Be careful not to let perfection drive your desire for success. We can strive to be the best at what we do but should consider that improvements will naturally come with time and practice. Do not let not having the perfect plan or idea stop you from beginning. Business ideas and things that impact our lives need to be carefully considered, however, it is easier to tailor a project that is in motion versus to one that doesn't exist. In other words, give God something to work with. If you never start, there is nothing to mold, redesign or modify.

WORD OF THE DAY

Perfectionist: A person who refuses to accept any standard short of perfection.

ACTIVITY 6

List 3 goals that you struggle with achieving because you do not have the perfect plan.

1. ______________________________

2. ______________________________

3. ______________________________

JOURNAL QUESTION: What areas of your life do you find yourself being a perfectionist?

READING RECOMMENDATION: Monica Ramirez Basco, Ph.D, Never Good Enough: Freeing Yourself from the Chains of Perfectionism (1999)

ACCOUNTABILITY DAY SEVEN

"Freedom is a return to the responsibility of stewardship."

-Myles Monroe

When you feel stuck in your job, career, home life or personal life, how long do you stay in that place mentally? It is easy to wallow when things don't go according to plan but there should be accountability for continuing the work in spite of hiccups. For instance, when things do not go according to plan, do not throw the entire plan away. Plans may be changed, or modified at any point and this should be a part of your "process." When you feel stuck, it is important to get the thoughts out of your head. Some of us wouldn't dare writing our thoughts onto paper for fear of what others would think if they read them. If this is you, understand that if thoughts are negative they will do you more harm than good if you internalize them. Write down negative thoughts, get them out of your head! If it helps keep a jar, note your negative thoughts and store them. For each negative thought that is stored, note one possible solution to ressolve the thought and store in a separate jar. Review your solutions as needed. Let your negative thoughts drive you into problem solving mode. Do not bring a problem, without bringing a solution. Appreciate the things that you do well and take note of them as you do challenges and barriers.

Please rate the following, on a scale of 1-10, I currently feel stuck in my career and/or personal goals. (Circle one) *Underline the area above that you feel stuck in (career or personal)*

1 2 3 4 5 6 7 8 9 10

WORD OF THE DAY

Accountability: Willingness to accept responsibility or account for one's actions.

ACTIVITY 7

Identify 3 areas of your life that you currently hold yourself accountable in and are a good steward.

1. ______________________________

2. ______________________________

3. ______________________________

JOURNAL QUESTION: How does your passion connect to areas of accountability in your life?

READING RECOMMENDATION: Timothy Butler, Getting Unstuck: How Dead Ends Become New Paths (2007)

GRATITUDE DAY EIGHT

"If we embrace our lot in life, count our blessings, and use what we have instead of complaining about what we don't have, we will have a good life."

-Joyce Meyer

Think about your role models growing up and your parental guidance. If during childhood you watched your parents practice good behavior, you will more than likely replicate it in your adulthood and with your own children. Likewise, if you watched your parents work tiressly to keep the ship afloat, take few financial risks, and give their all to others with little left over for themselves, this may also be your subconcious norm. While there isn't anything wrong with giving and sacrificing, sometimes it is the sacrificing of ourselves that leaves us lacking fulfillment. What is the balance for you? When you are juggling your personal and work life, what steps do you take to put yourself first? In general, do you find yourself complaining, or do you find yourself grateful?

While we may not get everything that we want in life, we all know someone that has a positive attitude, generally speaks good things and manages to practice gratefulness when things aren't that great. When mapping your plan to your passion, be sure to sprinkle in some patience and gratefulness. Find at least one person on the path that you are headed and link up with them. There are so many people in the world that are working towards where they want to be, and if this is you then you are not alone. Once you have found what inspires you, the path to success will become clearer.

WORD OF THE DAY

Gratitude: The state of being grateful; the quality of being thankful.

ACTIVITY 8

List 3 work related and 3 personal things/opportunities that you are grateful for.

1. ______________________________

2. ______________________________

3. ______________________________

JOURNAL QUESTION: Find the similarities and differences between the things listed above.

READING RECOMMENDATION: Joyce Meyer, The Power of Being Thankful: 365 Devotions for Discovering the Strength of Gratitude (2014)

PLAN
DAY NINE

"Ambition is the expression of your desire. It is the
fuel that gets you from point A to point B."

-Bob Proctor

Today's activity will require you to identify plans that you have made for yourself in the past. These plans may be work or personally related to the development of your success. Once you have identified these plans, consider the factors that drove them. Did you develop these plans based on your own personal wants and needs? Are there any past plans left incomplete that you would like to revisit in the upcoming months? Today's journal prompt will also require you to study past plans that were successfully executed. What was different about the plans that were executed successfully and those that were not? A plan cannot exist where there is no commitment and 1 hour of planning can save you many hours of doing. The 34th President of the United States, Dwight Eisenhower stated: "In preparing for battle I have always found that plans are useless but planning in indispensable." In other words, have a plan to work and work your plan. The word plan in itself is both a noun and a verb. For purposes of todays lesson, plan is a verb and action word. Once it has been developed, it should be executed.

Have you been consistent with seeing your life plans through to the end? What barriers have you allowed to interfere? Barriers and challenges are important because they help us when we are are ready to regroup. Challenges help us strategize regarding ways we can do things differently the second time around.

WORD OF THE DAY

Plan: An intention or decision about what one is going to do. A detailed proposal for doing or achieving something.

ACTIVITY 9

Identify 3 plans that you have developed to help you reach your financial goals.

1. ____________________

2. ____________________

3. ____________________

JOURNAL QUESTION: Compare and constrast past plans that were accomplished and those left unrealized. What works for you and what does not?

READING RECOMMENDATION: Tony Evans, Your Comeback: Your Past Doesn't Have to Determine Your Future (2018)

AUTOBIOGRAPHY DAY TEN

"In the end, it is the person you become, not the things you achieve, that is most important."

-Les Brown

If you had to write your autobiography today, would you be happy with it? Your task for today is to create a timeline in your journal in which you highlight major life events and accomplishments. Once your time line has been created, begin to draft the story. Were there any events that made you feel powerful or gave you a great sense of accomplishment? What was your favorite memory? Have you made the impact that you have wanted to in the world?

An autobiography isn't important just to "think" about. It is important for us to visualize and see. We must see our successess as well as our failures. Once you have your autobiography written, use it to plan. You can project another 20-30 years out and fill in what you would like to see happen in the future. While this may seem like a long shot, find someone currently living at the age in which you would like to see yourself one day. Ask them questions about their life and if they planned or not. Also ask them if there are any things they would have done differently and use their feedback as part of your planning and development process. Consider the major events that are currently a part of your story. How can you use them in a positive way? Remember, in your autobiography, it is important to establish who you are and who you are not. Identifying strengths and weaknessess help us to successfully execute our plans.

WORD OF THE DAY

Autobiography: An account of one's life as written by that person.

ACTIVITY 10

List 3 life events that you believe will/has pushed your toward your purpose.

1. ____

2. ____

3. ____

JOURNAL QUESTION: What is your favorite part of your autobiography and what would you change if you could? How do you see yourself moving forward?

READING RECOMMENDATION: John C. Maxwell, Put Your Dream to the Test: 10 Questions that Will Help You See It and Seize It (2011)

TENACITY
DAY ELEVEN

"If you are successful and have not suffered, someone has suffered for you, and if you are suffering without succeeding, perhaps someone may succeed after you. There is not success without suffering."

-John Maxwell

Now that you have written your autobiography, let's return to day one of this workbook. Recall that day one asked you to rank your current satisfaction with your job/career. Now that you have created a timeline of major life events and created an autobiography, please do the following: Take a look at your timeline and observe if there were periods of time career wise, that you were more on track than others. When considering your past jobs/careers pay close attention to major life events that occurred during that time frame that either knocked you off track or opened the door for new opportunities. Did you notice waves of progress or stagnation on your life timeline?

This workbook will engage you in the planning process for your next steps personally and career wise. Today's activity will require you to list 3 things that you will commit to doing that will transition you or prepare you for your desired job. If you currently have your desired job, today's activity will require you to identify 3 things that will grow you or push you to the next level. A good practice is to check-in and reflect every 3 months to assess your progress. Beyond the 21 days of journaling required for this workbook, set aside a time for journaling on a daily basis. Morning journaling may help to plan and structure your day; Evening journaling may help to gather thoughts for gratitude and reflection. Be sure not to break your appointment and commitment to yourself, even when it feels hard, uncomfortable or you simply lack motivation. Daily journaling will help you quickly observe what works and what doesn't work. It will also show you where to focus your energy.

WORD OF THE DAY

Tenacity: The quality of being able to grip something firmly; persistence, determination.

ACTIVITY 11

List 3 focus areas that you will commit to for the next 12 months to expand your career.

1. ____________________

2. ____________________

3. ____________________

JOURNAL QUESTION: What areas have you given up in that you should have persevered?

READING RECOMMENDATION: Angela Duckworth, GRIT: The Power of Passion and Perseverance (2016)

INTROSPECTION DAY TWELVE

"Accepting failure in the positive sense becomes effective when you believe that the right to fail is as important as the right to succeed."

-John Maxwell

Today is a day of introspection. How have you dealt with past failures in your life? No matter if the failures were personal or work related, what impact did they leave on your will, drive and motivation? If you discovered in days 1-11 that you are working a job and would like to move more towards a career, what steps will you take for this to happen? Likewise, if you discovered that you would like to shift careers and work in a field more in line with your passions, have you considered what that would look like? Developing a plan requires action steps. Instrospection and reflection are most imporant after experiencing failure. In fact, every failure should be looked at as a learning opportunity.

When developing your plan, be sure to keep track of all of your action steps. When it is time to rework your plan, relist the steps that were completed successfully. For each action that was experienced as failure, write down exactly what went wrong and what you will do differently the next time around. Hold yourself accountable for the "re-work" and improvement to your plan, no matter what. Commitment supersedes motivation. While motivation may not be felt each day, commitment and tenacity will help you to power through on days that you simply don't feel like it. We have all heard the phrase, do a little each day. No matter how big or small the effort, the important thing is that we keep persevering.

WORD OF THE DAY

Introspection: A reflection looking inward; self-observation, soul-searching. The examination or observation of one's own mental and emotional processes.

ACTIVITY 12

Self-reflect and identify 3 adjectives that describe who you are at your core.

1. ____________________

2. ____________________

3. ____________________

JOURNAL QUESTION: Who do you believe you are at your core, your "true self?" Does your timeline of life events/achievements support this belief and perception? Why or why not?

READING RECOMMENDATION: Steve Harvey, Jump: Take the Leap of Faith to Achieve Your Life of Abundance (2016)

DISCIPLINE DAY THIRTEEN

"Achieving worthwhile goals usually requires continuous, often repeated efforts."

-Michael Simpson

There is a saying that hard work beats talent when talent doesn't work hard. It is no secret that discipline and hardwork will bring us closer to achieving goals in any area in which we are not talented. This is because talent also requires us to develop our skills and properly demonstrate/display our abilities. Some people are ok without developing talents because they do not plan to use them on a larger scale. Others understand that discipline and commitment may yield the same result as talent. For example, any thing you practice daily you may become really good at. While we don't necessarily develop discipline for others, it does motivate others to see that anything is possible when you want it bad enough.

While intention is good, it ALONE does not yield progress. A person on the right track may get run over if they just sit there! We must persist in our goals and plans no matter what. Begin to identify small things that you are willing to do to reach your goals on a daily/weekly basis. Practice new habits and create a system of rewards for yourself (positive reinforcement). If you don't keep your commitments for the week, Do Not punish yourself. Speak positively over your life and give it a shot next week. You are not a failure, you can win, and you are a WINNER. Give yourself the grace and mercy to start again when needed.

WORD OF THE DAY

Discipline: To train or develop by instruction and exercise especially in self control.

ACTIVITY 13

Identify 3 areas in which your life could use a little more discipline.

1. ______________________________

2. ______________________________

3. ______________________________

JOURNAL QUESTION: How do you think the areas listed above impact your divine purpose?

READING RECOMMENDATION: Brian Tracy, No Excuses!: The Power of Self-Discipline; 21 Ways to Achieve Lasting Happiness and Success (2010)

GOAL DAY FOURTEEN

"The first key difference between an unmet goal and personal success is the belief that it can be achieved."

-Michael Hyatt

On day eleven of this workbook we listed 3 areas to focus on for the next 12 months. Today we will identify 3 goals for each focus area. Please note, it is up to you to decide if you will tackle all focus areas at once or devote time periods to each. For example, if you identified a financial focus area, you may identify a six month savings goal, investment goal or debt pay off goal. If your focus area is to transition careers, you might identify a certificate to obtain in the next three months or classes that you wish to complete towards your goal.

When setting your goals, keep in mind that they should be SMART goals. SMART goals are Specific, Measurable, Achievable, Realistic and Time based. SMART goals should be specific and identify the desired result (the who, what, when, where and how). Measurable goals should be numerically or descriptively quantifiable, for example, how will you track progress? Lastly, all SMART goals should be: Achievable, and include logical action steps; Realistic and align with your long term goals, purpose and areas of focus; and finally, they should always be Time-based. Be sure to create a time frame for when you want to accomplish all goals set. Remember, goals are set as a method to keep ourselves accountable and growing. While discipline requires us to govern our selves and master self control; goals help to keep us on track and responsible for the things that matter most in our lives.

WORD OF THE DAY

Goal: The object of a person's ambition or effort; an aim or desired result.

ACTIVITY 14

Take the focus areas from activity 11 and identify 3 goals for each one.

FOCUS AREA 1	FOCUS AREA 2	FOCUS AREA 3
Goal 1: ______________	Goal 1: ______________	Goal 1: ______________
Goal 2: ______________	Goal 2: ______________	Goal 2: ______________
Goal 3: ______________	Goal 3: ______________	Goal 3: ______________

JOURNAL QUESTION: What is your timeline for accomplishing goals set in each focus area?

READING RECOMMENDATION: Sarah Jakes Roberts, Don't Settle for Safe: Embracing the Uncomfortable to Become Unstoppable (2018)

Quarterly Action Step and Timeline Activity

Focus Area One	Action Steps/Milestones	Who	By When
	•		
	•		
	•		
	•		
	•		
Focus Area Two	**Action Steps/Milestones**	**Who**	**By When**
	•		
	•		
	•		
	•		
	•		
Focus Area Three	**Action Steps/Milestones**	**Who**	**By When**
	•		
	•		
	•		
	•		
	•		

Exercise: As a supplement to day 14, please take a moment to complete action steps for your SMART goals and areas of focus. Use this page as a resource and duplicate as needed quarterly.

SELF-TALK DAY FIFTEEN

"Be Mindful of your self-talk. It's a conversation with the universe."

-David James Lees

If you have read the book, "The Secret" or at least heard of it, then you know it is based on the law of attraction and the principle that our thoughts can change the world directly. You may have a behavior that you would like to change or outcome that you would like to achieve but do not understand why producing results is so difficult for you. For the next 7 days, I would like for you to try something different. Focus on your thoughts for the next 7 days. Focus on positive thinking. If it helps, read the positive thoughts from day 7 in the morning and in the evening before you go to bed. What you may notice after 7 days is that it may be easier to change your thinking then to change your behavior outright. Change your mind and your behavior will follow.

If our thoughts manifest and impact the world around us, consider how your self-talk may be undoing the goals that you are trying to reach each day. For example, we may set a goal to have more meaningful and positive interactions with the people that we work with, but our body language may indirectly communicate our self-talk. People may pick up on our thoughts or sense that something is off or that we are being disingenuine. We must be genuine and authentic with ourselves if we want our goals and dreams to manifest. If your partner could sit in on your self-talk, what would they say? Do you celebrate the small victories in your life or are you your harshest critic?

Do you give yourself space and opportunity to learn from your mistakes or do you judge yourself? Be kind to yourself ALWAYS.

WORD OF THE DAY

Self-talk: The act or practice of talking to oneself, either aloud or silently and mentally.

ACTIVITY 15

List three negative or deep rooted thoughts that you would change immediately if you could.

1. ______________________________

2. ______________________________

3. ______________________________

JOURNAL QUESTION: How has self-talk impacted your ability to accomplish your goals?

READING RECOMMENDATION: Rhonda Byrne, The Secret (2006)

CRITICISM DAY SIXTEEN

"You've been criticizing yourself for years, and it hasn't worked. Try approving of yourself and see what happens."

-Louise Hay

Negative thoughts and criticism can keep us off track far longer than ever anticipated. The life goals that we set for ourselves will always require positive reinforcement. Afterall, it isnt the positive thoughts and progress that block us from achieving our goals. It is our negative self-talk and hidden beliefs that hinder our ability to succeed.

Now that you have learned to practice positive self talk, make a list of language that you can utilize daily to boost your confidence and motivate you to reach your goals. You may utilize positive affirmations but make sure that the language specifically ties into the goals that you identified on day 14. Try statements that will help you get back on track instead of self destructive thoughts. For example, "I can't get back time, but I can get back on track" or "I am human, it is ok to have a meltdown, but today I will refocus on where I am headed." Find music, poetry or inspirational messages to listen to in your car or at work that will keep you focused on success daily. Remember that fear and perfection are the greatest enemies of success. If you find yourself focused on fear of failure, remember that your will to persevere is often the difference between failure and success. Our will to succeed can withstand any fear we may be experiencing! Remember that "Many of life's perceived failures are by people who did not realize how close they were to success when they gave up (Thomas Edison)."

WORD OF THE DAY

Criticism: Expression of disapproval of someone or something based on perceived faults.

ACTIVITY 16

List 3 positive affirmations that will counteract self-criticism and keep you on track.

1. ____________________

2. ____________________

3. ____________________

JOURNAL QUESTION: How can you turn your criticisms of yourself into positive language?

READING RECOMMENDATION: Steve Harvey, Act Like A Success, Think Like a Success: Discovering Your Gift and the Way to Life's Riches (2015)

EXERCISE: Please List 8 Affirmations that you will use to silence your inner critic.

POSITIVE AFFIRMATION ACTIVITY

-
-
-
-
-
-
-
-

Exercise: Please List 8 Affirmations that you will use to silence your inner critic.

PURPOSE
DAY SEVENTEEN

"The meaning of life is to find your gift.
The purpose of life is to give it away."
-Pablo Picasso

No one was created to live in a silo or vacuum. If you have not figured out your purpose by now, you must put yourself out there! While this may seem a little bit scary at first, it is the only way to manifest the law of attraction. You must become the person that you think about, and you can start by doing a little each day. When discovering your life's purpose, it is important to get out and try new things. A suggestion is to get out and try all those things you've thought you might enjoy but never got around to doing.

Today's activity will require you to plan for new experiences. This is your time to be bold, your time to take risks and your time to be limitless. This is your time to try the ideas that everyone told you that you could not do. Earlier on in this work book we discussed the importance of having an accountability partner. It is important to note that your partner is there to encourage and support, you do not need their approval! It is ok to try something new just for you and not for the approval of others. Need some ideas? Take a finance class, learn to play an instrument, volunteer at a local church or community center. The goal is to add at least one new experience to your calendar each month and do what it takes to fulfill that commitment to yourself. While you are out experiencing life, you might meet someone on a similar path with similar interests. It just might be the breakthrough that you needed to take you to your next level.

WORD OF THE DAY

Purpose: The reason for which something is done or created; one's intent or objective.

ACTIVITY 17

List 3 new experiences that you would like to have that you have been afraid to try.

1. ______________________________

2. ______________________________

3. ______________________________

JOURNAL QUESTION: What fears have you faced as associated with the activity above?

READING RECOMMENDATION: Oprah Winfrey, What I Know For Sure (2014)

NEW EXPERIENCES GOALS

■	My Plan: Date Completed:
■	My Plan: Date Completed:
■	My Plan: Date Completed:
■	My Plan: Date Completed:
■	My Plan: Date Completed:
■	My Plan: Date Completed:
■	My Plan: Date Completed:

Please use this page to note additional experiences that you want to have, and write your plan for doing them. Go back once they have been completed and journal about your experience. Keep in mind that this is a living document and you may make changes or add new ideas as they come to you. Highlight the activities that bring you joy once complete. Eliminate those you would never do again.

FOCUS
DAY EIGHTEEN

"The Fears We Don't Face Become Our Limits."

-Robin Sharma

Any business owner will tell you that the secret to success and a better business is focus. You must choose your path and carefully focus. When we are focused on several ideas at once, our core ideas and business plans may become diluted. Remember, opportunities tend to carry most excitement when they are new. You may be focused on a business plan that has hit a rough patch. When this happens, it is sometimes more difficult to focus and work through the rough patch than it is to try something new altogether. There will always be new opportunities. See your ideas through until the end before closing the chapter and choosing another path.

Often times, too many ideas and opportunities may cause those of us seeking purpose to freeze altogether, unable to pursue a path for fear of choosing the wrong one. Today's activity will take into account that we often have multiple interests. You have already identified areas that you will be focusing on in the upcoming months on day 14. The worksheet on the following page will allow you to chart any other interests and opportunities for exploration that may arise during the activity dedicated toward working on your goals. This worksheet can be used to chart other possibilities and to look for alternative ideas that are a natural match for each other. New ideas are great, and naturally we will not be laser focused every moment. Set completely separate ideas aside for a later date, you can always return to them, I promise.

WORD OF THE DAY

Focus: The state or quality of having or producing clear visual definition.

ACTIVITY 18

List 3 solutions for getting back on track when you've wondered off the beaten path.

1. ____

2. ____

3. ____

JOURNAL QUESTION: What eminent thoughts and challenges do you face after losing focus?

READING RECOMMENDATION: Rob Fazio, PhD, Simple Is the New Smart: 26 Success Strategies to Build Confidence, Inspire Yourself, and Reach Your Ultimate Potential (2016)

SOMEDAY PLANS, IDEAS & INTERESTS

-
-
-
-
-
-
-

Exercise: Create a list of future projects. This list should include the projects and plans that you want to do, but not right now. Much like your new experiences list, this is a living document where you'll record every new project that crosses your mind, especially when you've wondered off track.

CHARACTER DAY NINETEEN

"Knowledge will give you power, but
character will give you respect."
-Bruce Lee

As we have gotten closer to determining our purpose, we have identified the following: (1) Areas of focus for the upcoming months, (2) New Experiences that we would like to try, and (3) Our Someday List of Interests. Once the lists have been created, please create check in points for yourself. Some of us may use our lists daily, others weekly, monthly, etc. Find a system that works for you and implement accordingly. For today's activity you will compare the three lists that you have created and make a list of the characteristics/qualities of people that you might find engaging in the activities that you listed. You might realize that your "New Experience" list activities require you to be a "risk taker", your "Area of Focus" list requires you to be more disciplined and your "Someday List of Future Interests" requires you to be more open minded.

Your personal qualities and characteristics are a good gauge for whether or not you will enjoy the activities identified on days 17 and 18 of this workbook. Keep in mind, the goal is for you to compare and contrast all of the exploratory activities, noting exactly what you did like about your new experiences and what you did not like. If new hobbies arise out of the exploratory component of this workbook, determine if those qualities are linked to your passion. In addition to this exercise, the supplemental activity on the next page may help you identify that types of people that you draw close to and connect with. Imagine, the person that you are closest with and think about their unique characteristics. How you would describe them as individuals and how you are similar? Do you share characteristics?

WORD OF THE DAY

Character: The mental and moral qualities distinctive to an individual.

ACTIVITY 19

List 3 characteristics that you have in common with the closest individual in your life.

1. ______________________________

2. ______________________________

3. ______________________________

JOURNAL QUESTION: What does your character say about you? Are you who you want to be?

READING RECOMMENDATION: Stephen R. Covey, The 7 Habits of Highly Effective People: Powerful Lessons in Personal Change (2004)

Venn Diagram Activity

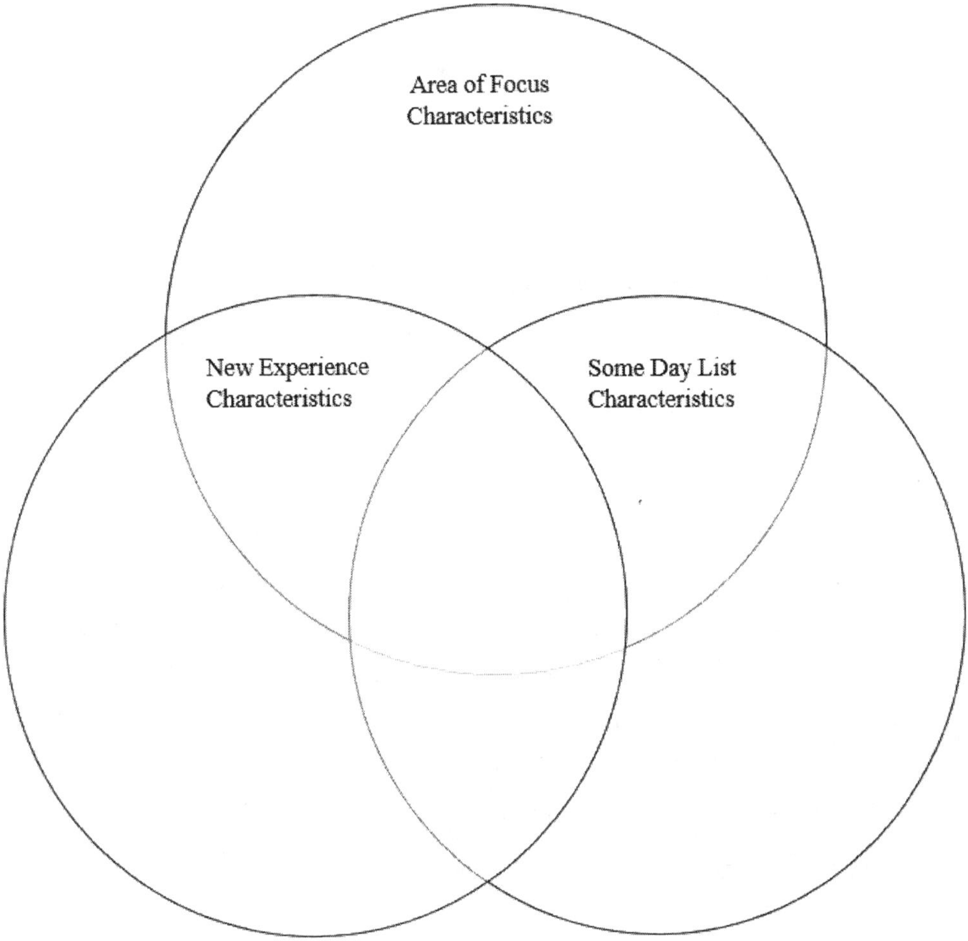

Exercise: Please use the Venn Diagram to enter characteristics that individuals in your 3 lists (Areas of focus, Someday Interests and New Experiences Goals) will display. Be sure to note overlapping characteristics.

DESTINY DAY TWENTY

"Your Life Has Purpose. Your Story is Important.
Your Dreams Count. Your Voice Matters.
You Were Born To Make An Impact."

-Zig Ziglar

If you haven't realized by day 20, it is important to note that your purpose is ONLY for you! It isn't to please anyone else and is specifically tied to your personal mission statement. Now that you have completed activities 1-19, your job is to create or revise your personal mission statement. Your statement should include your intentions, and actions that lead you towards your purpose. Be careful not to include the expectations of others in your mission statement, rather, carefully reflect on your mission using the activities from this workbook and your journal entries. Clear your mind and take some time to visualize yourself living and walking in your purpose. Meditate on your vision, how will you look, how will you feel? What positive benefits will walking in your purpose have on those around you? Remember, visualization is a part of the law of attraction.

When developing your personal mission statement, never downplay yourself or your abilities. Be positive, ambitious and realistic. Author Steven Covey, indicates in The 7 Habits of Highly Effective People that successful people are proactive and begin with the end in mind. Mission statements help to keep us on track and focused. They provide a gauge and tool for measurement. We can always take a look at our actions and ask ourselves how they tie into to our personal mission statements. If they don't, we can reprioritize both our time and actions around activities that speak to and fulfill our purpose. What will your legacy be? Will you fulfill your destiny?

WORD OF THE DAY

Destiny: The hidden power believed to control what will happen in the future; fate.

ACTIVITY 20

Identify 3 ways you would use your life to impact the world if you could.

1. ______________________________

2. ______________________________

3. ______________________________

JOURNAL ACTIVITY: Create a word cloud and develop your own personal mission statement.

READING RECOMMENDATION: T.D. Jakes, Destiny: Step Into Your Purpose (2016)

PERSEVERANCE DAY TWENTY ONE

"Perfection is an illusion and those who seek perfection
will find themselves unfulfilled their whole lives."
-Edwin Bliss

Today will require you to look back over your journal entries, autobiography, goals and new experiences lists. Take several different color highlighters and begin to highlight themes that you find in different colors. Take notes from your entries and circle the things that stand out to you. Treat your journal like a text book, write in the margin, circle, underline and highlight. The journal should be used not only for recording but also for notetaking. Themes that arise in your journal may reflect strengths, weaknesses and interests. Fitness, improving quality of life, investing in others, simplifying processes, children and missionary work may be examples of possible themes. While we have used this workbook to discover our purpose by focusing on our strengths and the things that we do well, we can also highlight challenges, barriers or areas that we find we need to improve upon. Use your journal as a living document. If you ever feel stuck return to it and regroup. The goal is always progress, not perfection.

Please indicate the following, on a scale of 1-10, after completing this workbook I feel more confident about my purpose and am committed to doing the work to fulfill it.

1 2 3 4 5 6 7 8 9 10

WORD OF THE DAY

Perseverance: Persistence in doing something despite difficulty or delay in achieving success.

ACTIVITY 21

Now that you have used this workbook and your journal to identify emerging themes in your life, list 3 career choices that fit your personality, character and strengths.

1. ____

2. ____

3. ____

JOURNAL QUESTION: Reflect on your 21-day process, what have you discovered about yourself?

READING RECOMMENDATION: Nancy Lynn Roberts, Progress Not Perfection: A Meaningful Journey with Lasting Joy (2012)

"Talk to yourself like you would to someone you love."

-Brene Brown

A Note From the Author

Congratulations on completing this workbook. Hopefully, now you are much further along in your journey of self-discovery. This workbook was created as part of a much needed self care regimen. As a working professional, the juggle of balancing self, family and career can be challenging at best. It almost requires us to be master prioritizers and even then we still may not be 100% comfortable with where we are focusing our time, talent and attention. We have to consider who ultimately suffers when we are not working in our purpose and walking towards our destiny.

After completing this workbook, hopefully you have identified areas you will commit to working harder at. Additionally, I hope you identified ways to celebrate the small successes, not to beat yourself up, and to get back on track when you feel frustrated and ready to throw in the towel. Your next steps are to implement and update your action plan quarterly. Feel free to replicate the "Quarterly Action Step and Timeline" activity for accountability purposes. You may actually want to separate out action steps and milestone achievements. Create action steps as part of the planning process, and return to the activity once the quarter has ended to record your milestones and progress.

Always remember, you can do anything that you put your time to and your mind to and that you matter!

Celebrate Your Success Always,

Dr. Lorena J.

REFERENCES

Bliss, E. C. (1991). *Getting things done: The ABCs of time management.* Charles Scribner's Sons.

Brown, B. (2008). *I thought it was just me (but it Isn'T): Telling the truth about perfectionism, inadequacy and power.* Gotham Books.

Brown, L. (1992). *Live your dreams: Say "YES" to life.* William Morrow & Co.

Carnegie, D. (2008). *The leader in you: How to win friends, influence people and succeed in a changing world.* Simon & Schuster.

Covey, S. R. (2013). *How to develop your personal mission statement.* FranklinCovey.

Covey, S. R. (2017). *The 7 habits of highly effective people: Powerful lessions in personal change.* DC Books.

Dictionary by Merriam-Webster: America's most-trusted online dictionary. (n.d.). Merriam-webster.com. Retrieved October 14, 2022, from https://www.merriam-webster.com/

Good News Network. (2021, October 25). *"The meaning of life is to find your gift. The purpose of life is to give it away." – Pablo Picasso (born 140 years ago).* Good News Network. https://www.goodnewsnetwork.org/picasso-quote-about-meaning-and-purpose/

Hay, L. (2002). *You can heal your life companion book.* Hay House.

Hill, N. (2008). *How to own your own mind.* Tarcherperigee.

Hyatt, M. (2018). *Your best year ever: A 5-step plan for achieving your most important goals.* Baker Books.

Jakes, T. D. (2008). *Life overflowing: 6 pillars for abundant living*. Bethany House Publishers.

Lee, B. (n.d.). *A quote by Bruce Lee*. Goodreads.com. Retrieved October 14, 2022, from https://www.goodreads.com/quotes/506371-knowledge-will-give-you-power-but-character-respect

Lees, D. J. (2015). *Wu wei wisdom*. Wu Wei Wisdom Ltd.

Lucado, M. (2015). *God is with you every day*. Thomas Nelson.

Maxwell, J. C. (2014). *How high will you climb?: Determine your success by cultivating the right attitude*. HarperCollins Leadership.

Meyer, J. (2005). *Attitudes of the mind: Change your outlook... Change Your Life*. Joyce Meyer Ministries.

Monroe, M. (2001). *Burden of freedom: Discover the keys to your individual and national freedom*. Charisma House.

Proctor, B. (2018). *It's not about the money*. G&D Media.

Sharma, R. (2018). *The 5 am club: Own your morning. Elevate your life*. HarperCollins.

Simpson, M. K., Sullivan, M., & Saddler, K. (2020). *Unlocking potential, second edition: 7 Coaching skills that transform individuals, teams, and organizations*. AmazonCrossing.

Wikipedia contributors. (2022, October 5). *Main Page*. Wikipedia, The Free Encyclopedia. https://en.wikipedia.org/w/index.php?title=Main_Page&oldid=1114291180

Word of the day. (n.d.). Dictionary.com. Retrieved October 14, 2022, from https://www.dictionary.com/

Ziglar, Z. (2008). *How to stay motivated: Developing the qualities of success*. Made for Success.